PUZZLE
WRIGHT
JUNIOR

JUNIOR New York

An Imprint of Sterling Publishing Co., Inc.
1166 Avenue of the Americas
New York, NY 10036

ISBN 978-1-4549-3153-9

Distributed in Canada by Sterling Publishing, Co., Inc.
c/o Canadian Manda Group, 664 Annette Street
Toronto, Ontario, Canada M6S 2C8
Distributed in the United Kingdom by GMC Distribution Services
Castle Place, 166 High Street, Lewes, East Sussex, England BN7 1XU
Distributed in Australia by NewSouth Books,
University of New South Wales, Sydney, NSW 2052, Australia

For information about custom editions, special sales, and premium and
corporate purchases, please contact Sterling Special Sales at 800-805-5489
or specialsales@sterlingpublishing.com.

Manufactured in Canada
Lot #:
2 4 6 8 10 9 7 5 3 1
04/19

Cover design by Valerie Hou

sterlingpublishing.com
puzzlewright.com

Introduction

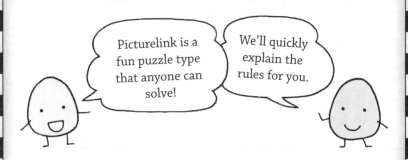

Picturelink is a fun puzzle type that anyone can solve!

We'll quickly explain the rules for you.

To solve a picturelink, simply draw lines to connect every pair of identical pictures with each other, as shown below.

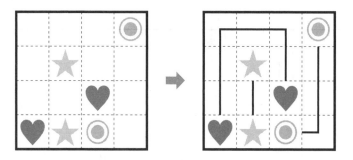

There are a few rules to keep in mind, though. Turn the page and we'll tell you more!

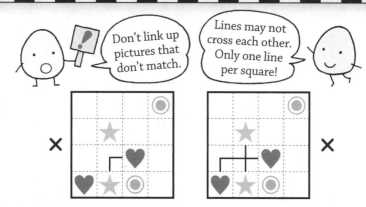

Now let's solve the puzzle all the way through.

The next four puzzles are practice puzzles and will give you hints to get you started. (After that, you're on your own.) Happy solving!

nikoli PUZZLE

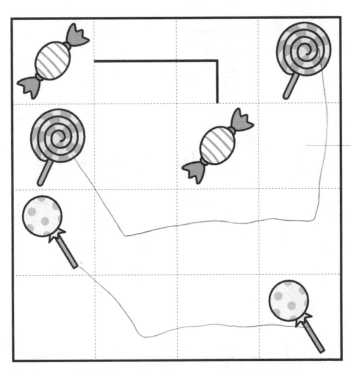

One pair of pictures has been connected for you.
How can you link up the other two?

Answer, page 84

Remember that the lines connecting matching pairs can't go diagonally or pass through other pictures.

Answer, page 84

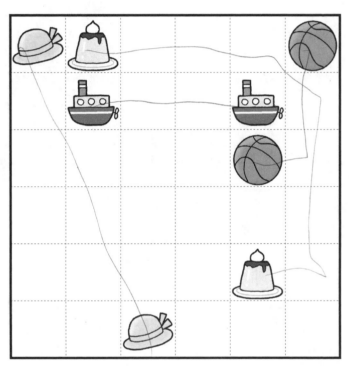

The key to this one is connecting the boats without blocking any other pairs of pictures.

Answer, page 84

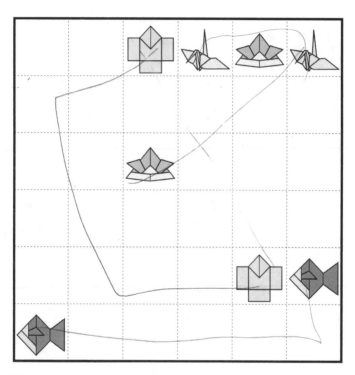

The two cranes in the top row are the trickiest pair to connect. Try starting with the fish first.

Answer, page 84

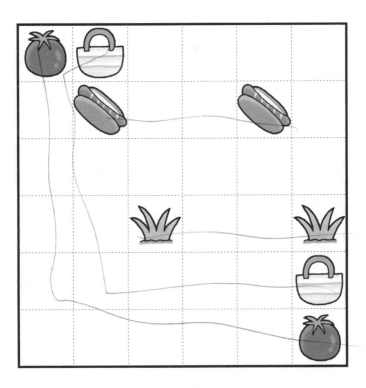

Answer, page 84

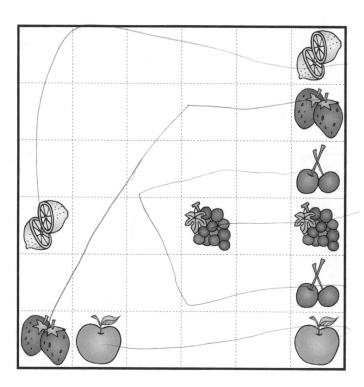

Answer, page 84

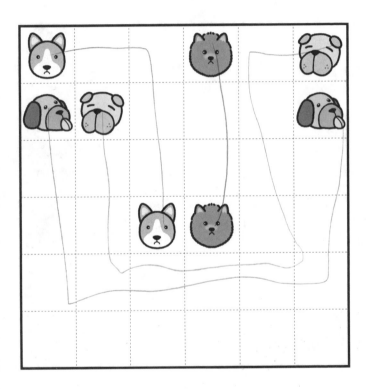

Answer, page 85

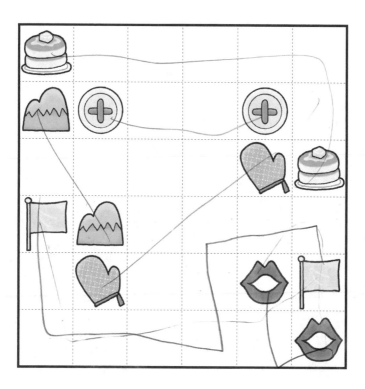

Answer, page 85

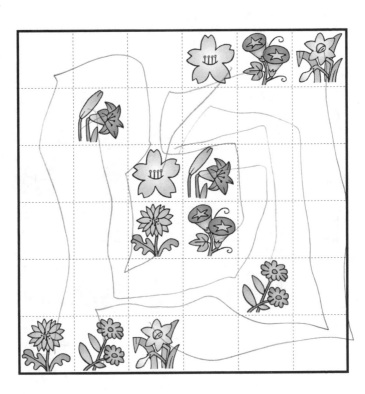

Answer, page 85

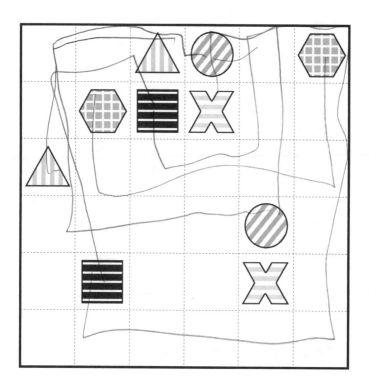

Answer, page 85

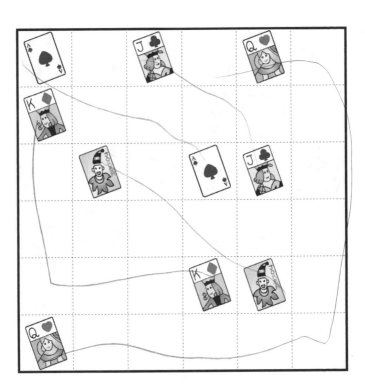

Answer, page 85

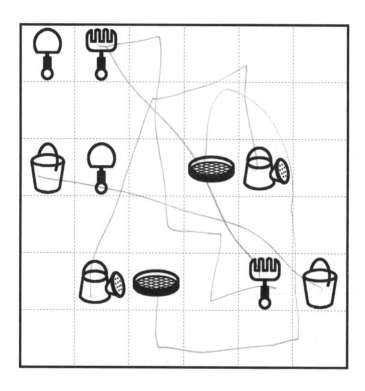

Answer, page 85

Answer, page 86

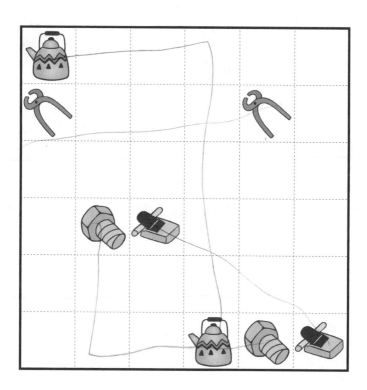

Answer, page 86

-19-

15

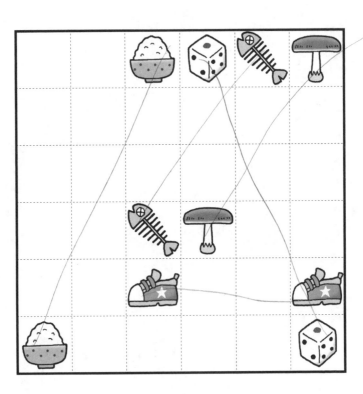

Answer, page 86

-20-

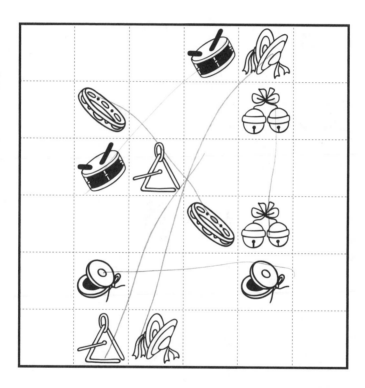

Answer, page 86

Answer, page 86

Answer, page 86

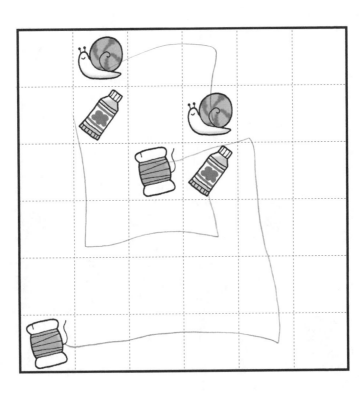

Answer, page 87

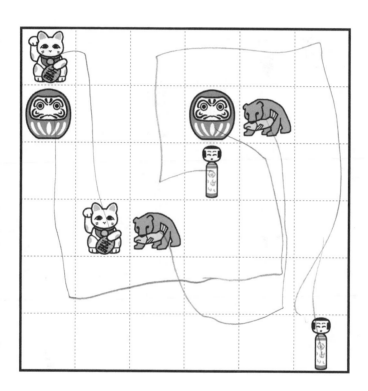

Answer, page 87

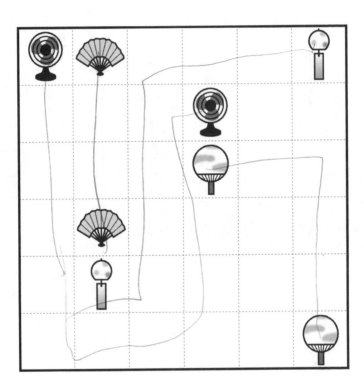

Answer, page 87

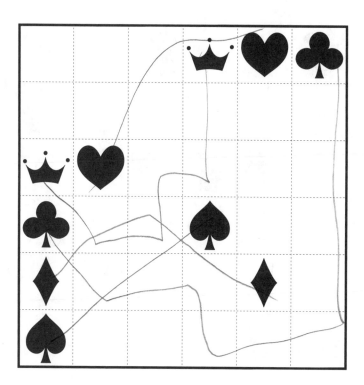

Answer, page 87

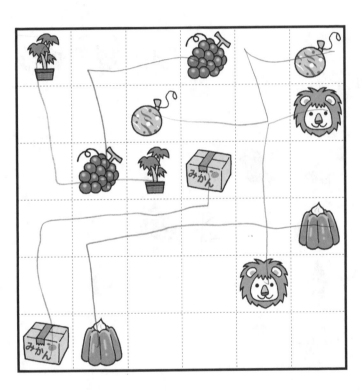

Answer, page 87

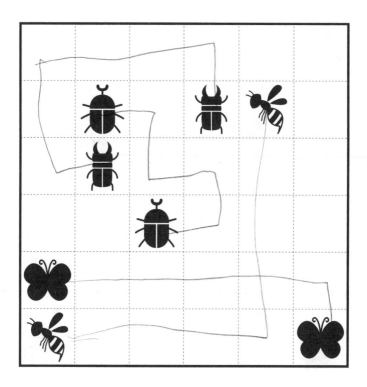

Answer, page 87

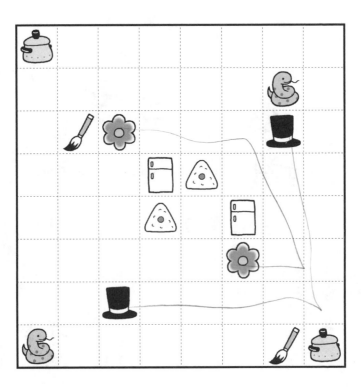

Answer, page 88

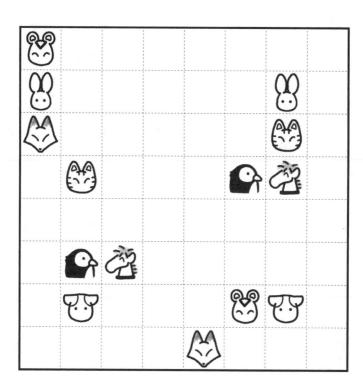

26

Answer, page 88

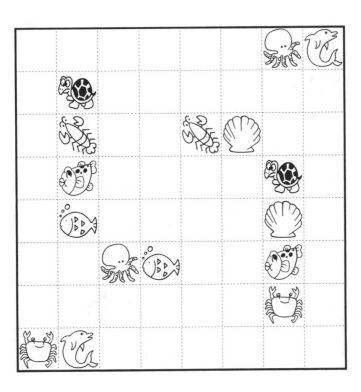

Answer, page 88

Answer, page 88

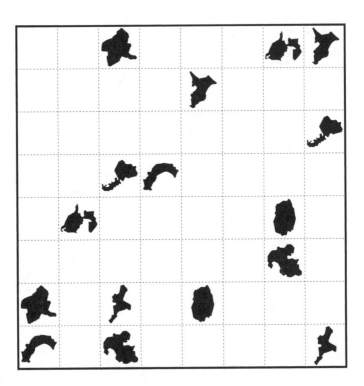

Answer, page 88

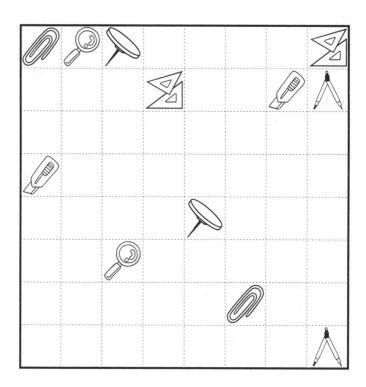

Answer, page 88

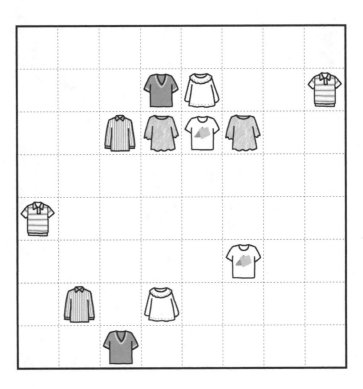

Answer, page 89

Answer, page 89

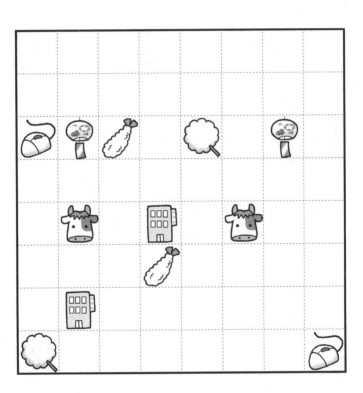

Answer, page 89

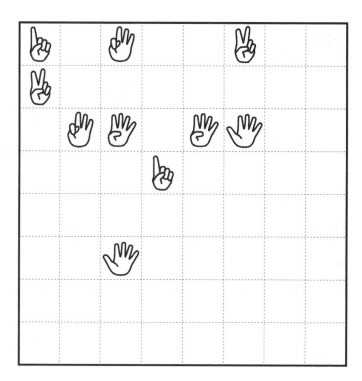

Answer, page 89

35

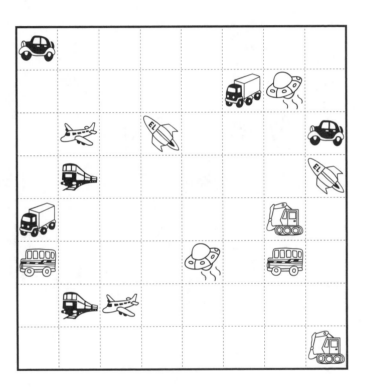

Answer, page 89

-40-

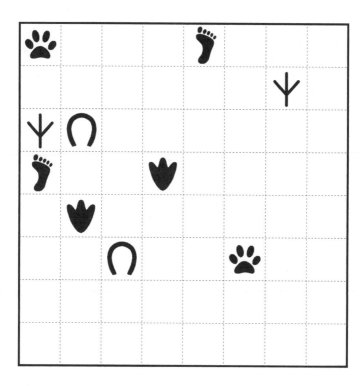

Answer, page 89

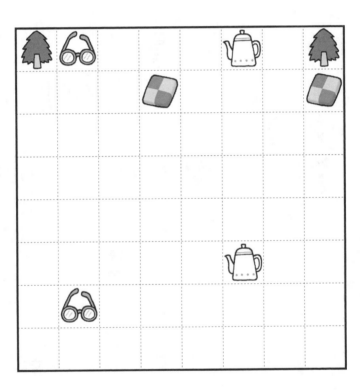

Answer, page 90

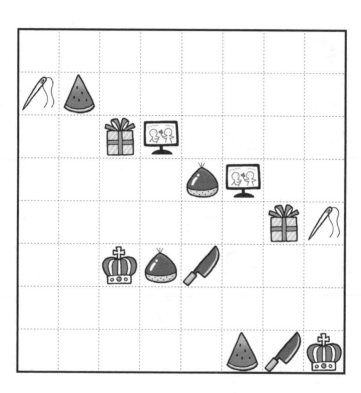

Answer, page 90

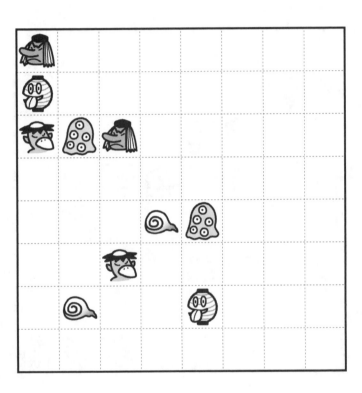

Answer, page 90

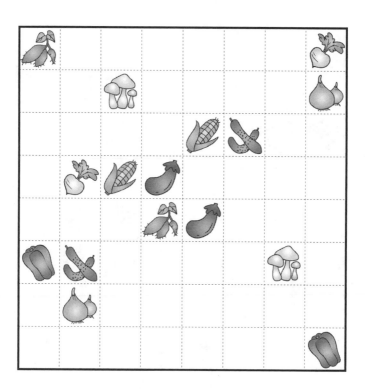

Answer, page 90

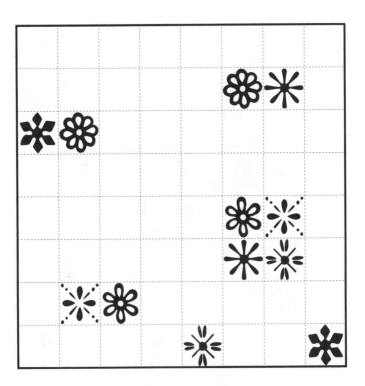

Answer, page 90

Answer, page 90

43

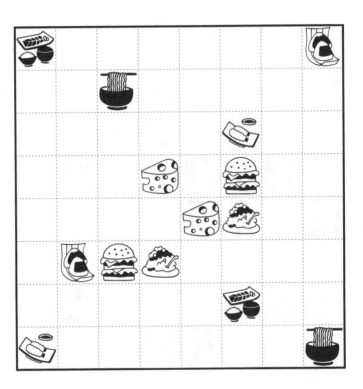

Answer, page 91

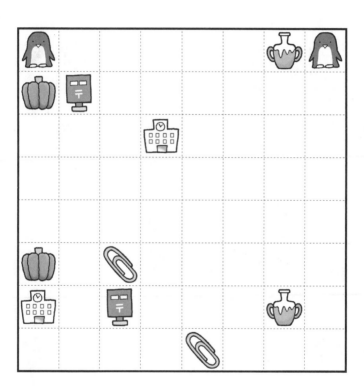

Answer, page 91

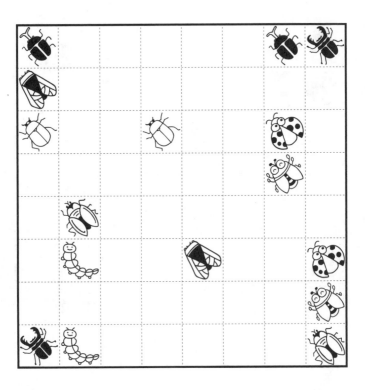

Answer, page 91

Answer, page 91

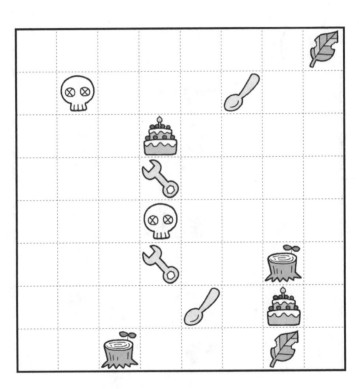

Answer, page 91

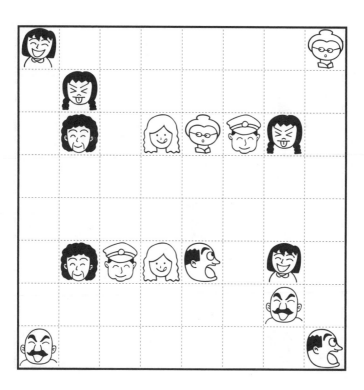

Answer, page 91

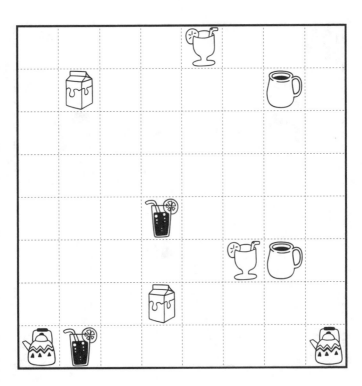

Answer, page 92

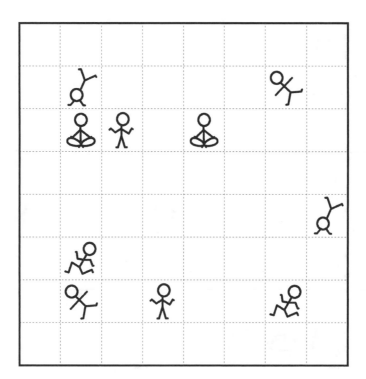

Answer, page 92

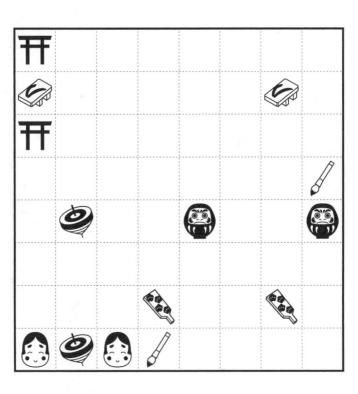

Answer, page 92

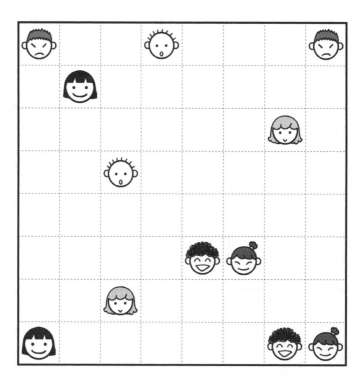

Answer, page 92

Answer, page 92

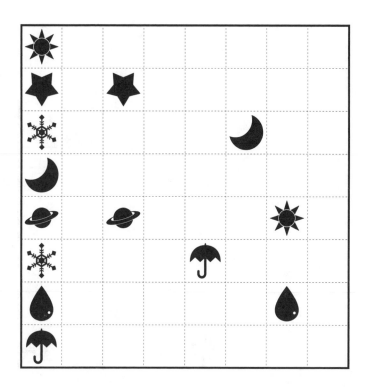

Answer, page 92

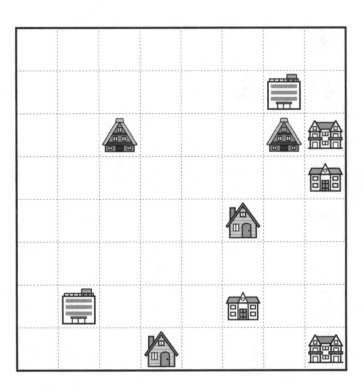

Answer, page 93

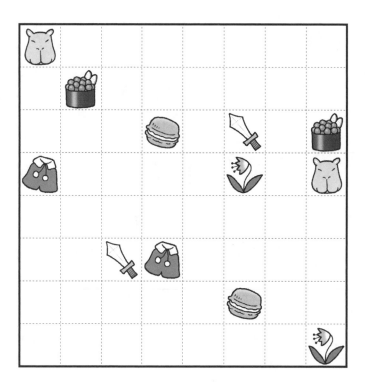

Answer, page 93

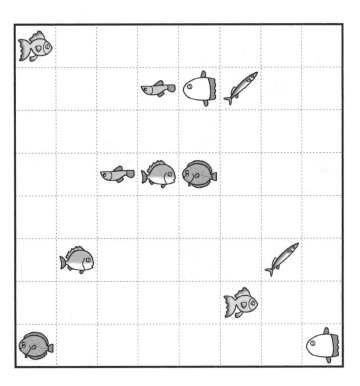

Answer, page 93

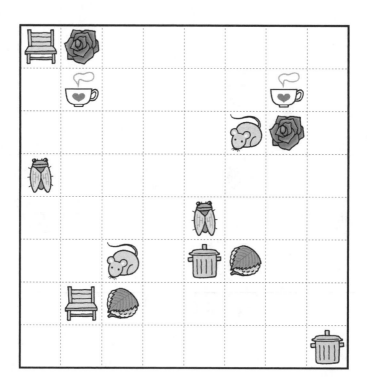

Answer, page 93

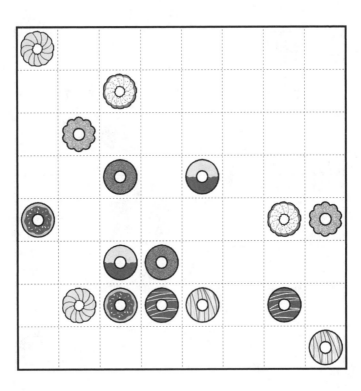

Answer, page 93

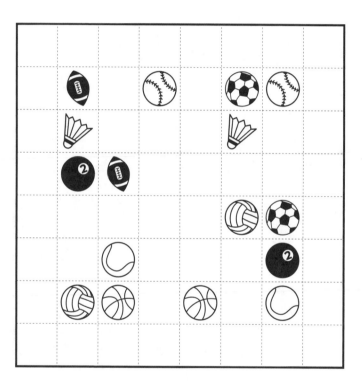

			3	1			
4						4	5
5							
6						7	
	6						
							8
							3
7	8						2
			2	1			

Answer, page 94

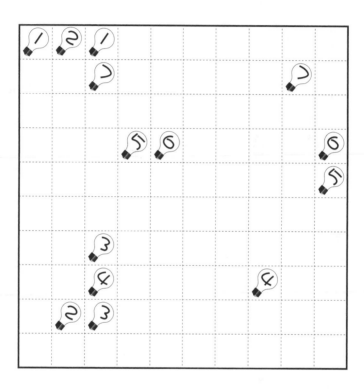

Answer, page 94

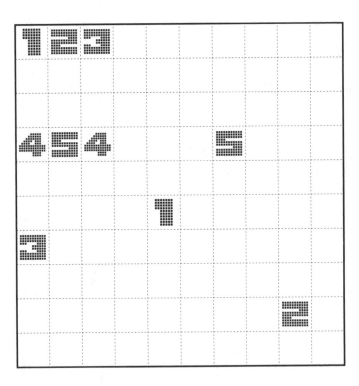

Answer, page 94

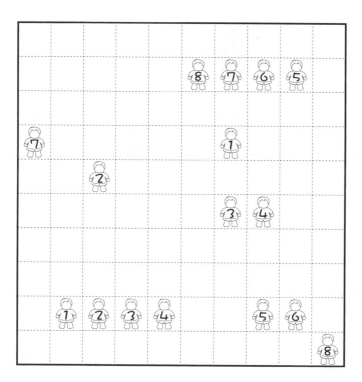

Answer, page 94

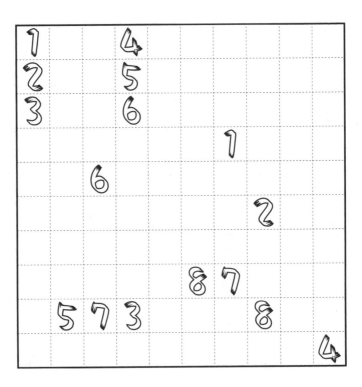

Answer, page 94

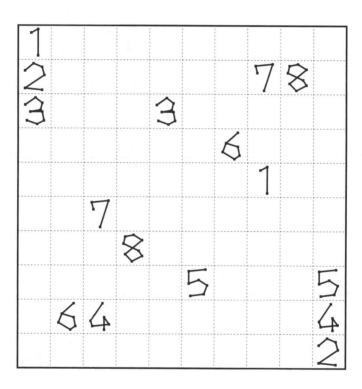

Answer, page 94

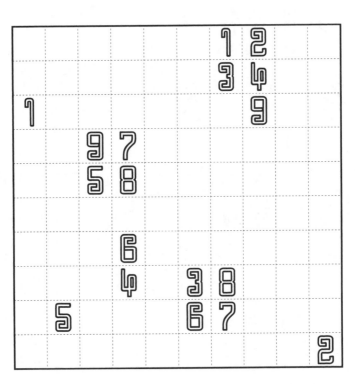

Answer, page 95

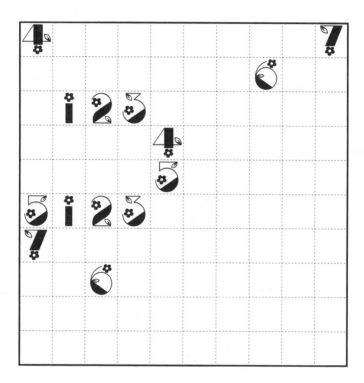

Answer, page 95

1	2		4	5				
	3		6					
		4		7				
		2	5	8				
			3				6	
	9							
							9	
		1	8	7				

Answer, page 95

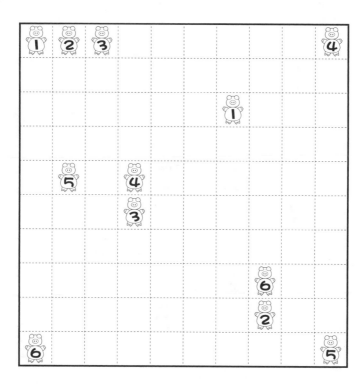

Answer, page 95

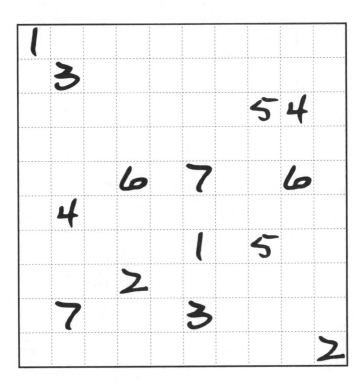

Answer, page 95

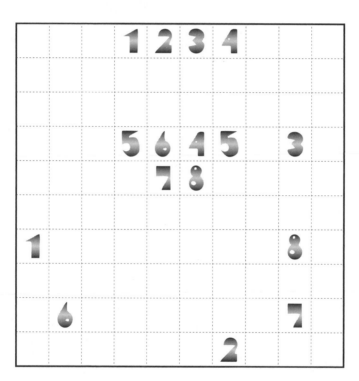

Answer, page 95

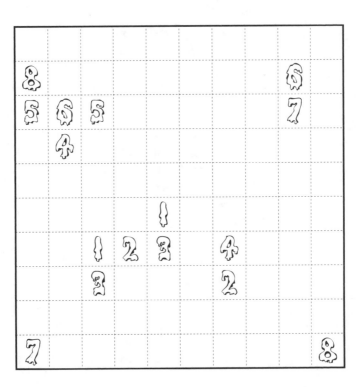

Answer, page 96

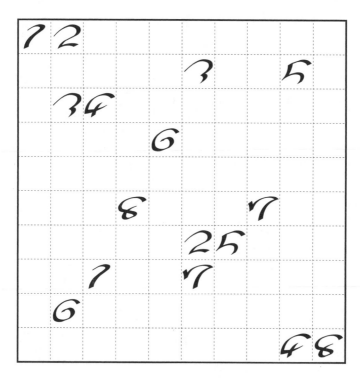

Answer, page 96

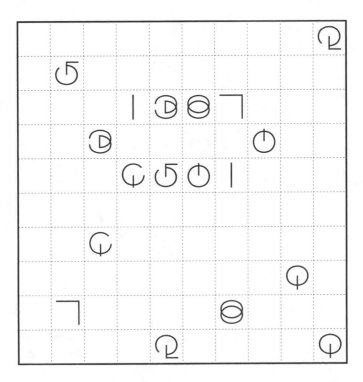

Answer, page 96

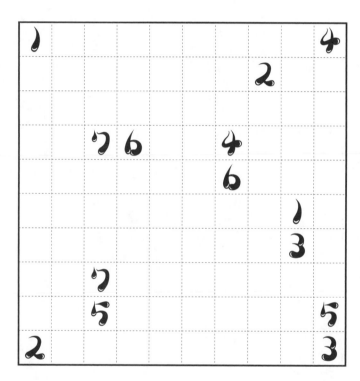

Answer, page 96

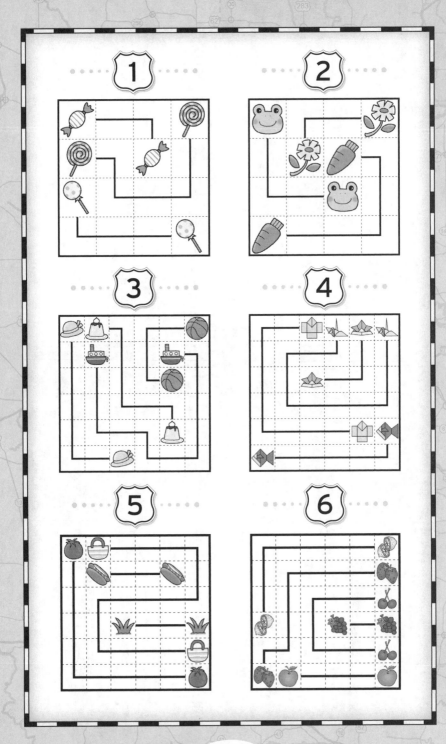

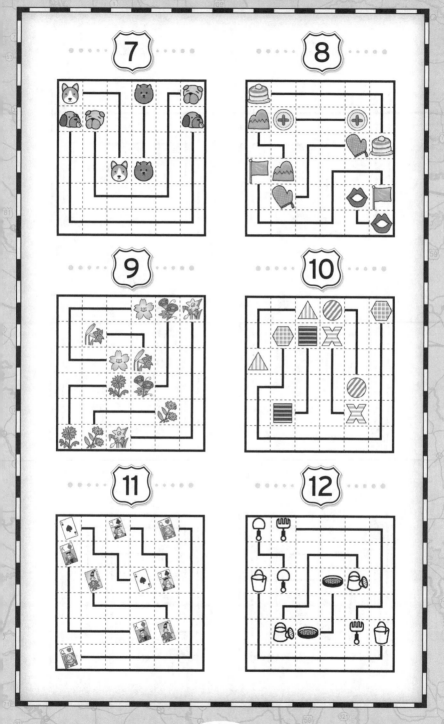

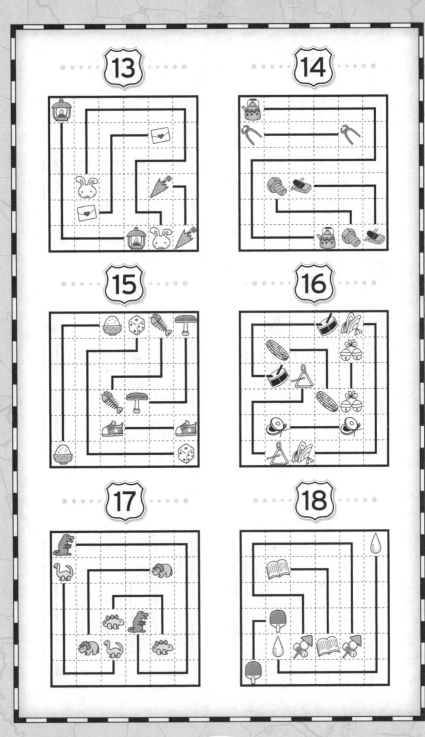

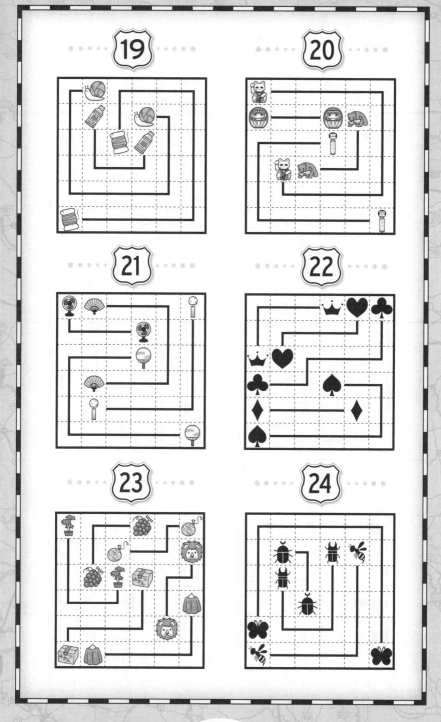

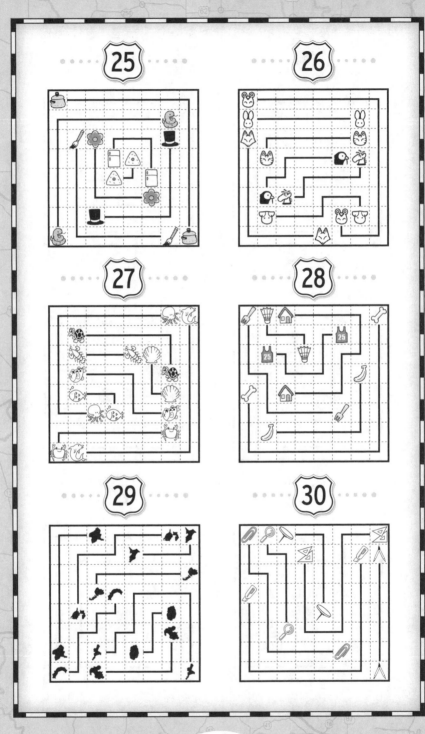

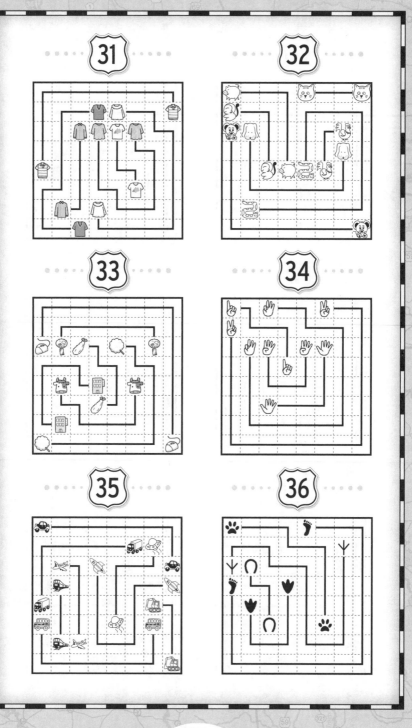

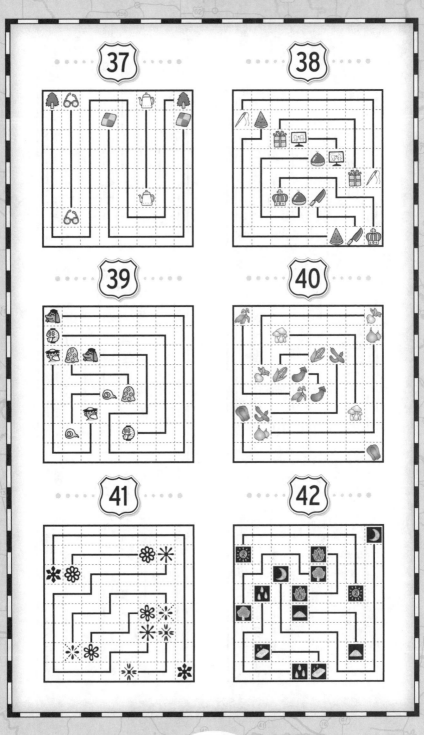

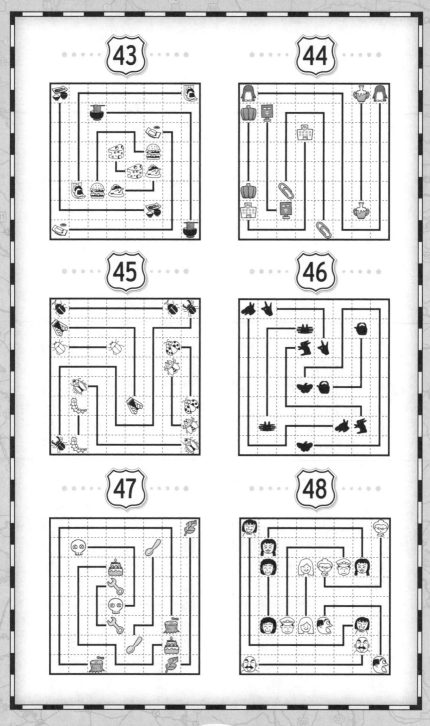

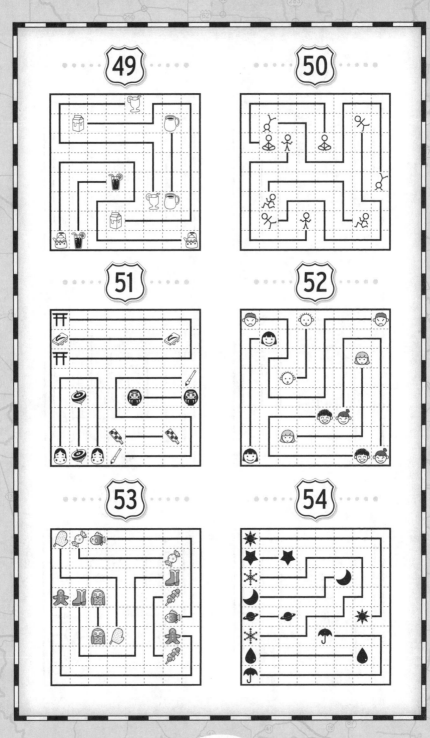

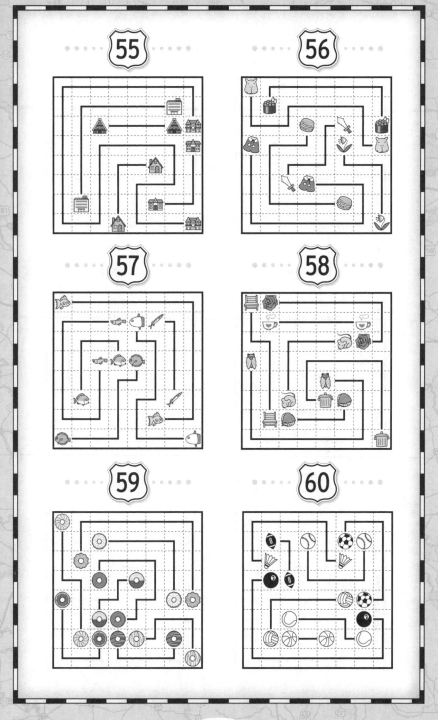

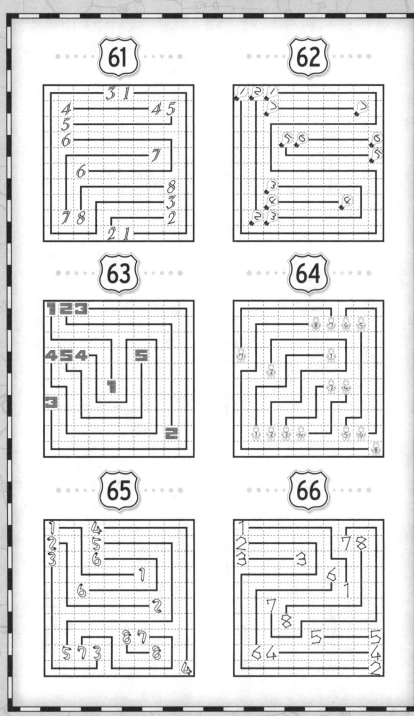

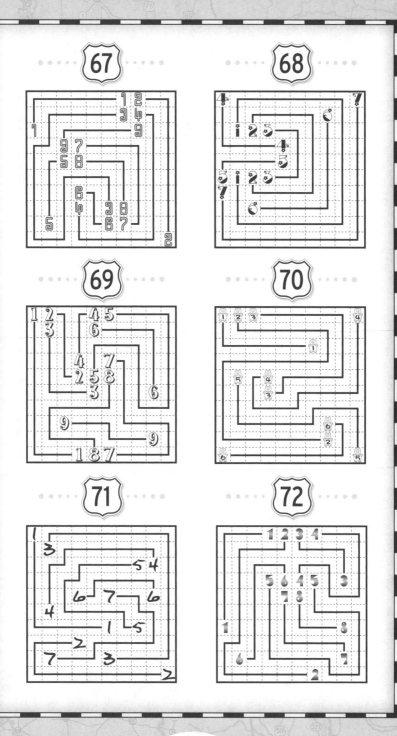

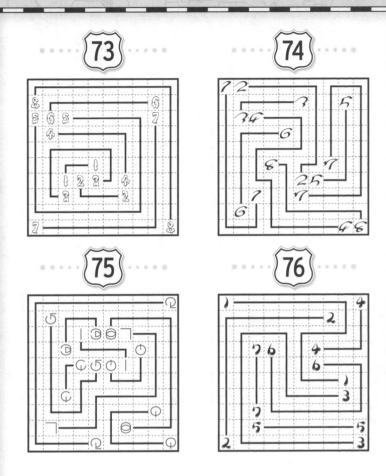